Sept 2018

Thank you  part of our Wolfpack these two days!

Wendy Carolyn

WOLFPACK

Also by Abby Wambach

Forward: A Memoir

WOLFPACK

How to Come Together,
Unleash Our Power,
and Change the Game

Abby Wambach

CELADON
BOOKS
—
NEW YORK

www.celadonbooks.com

ISBN 978-1-250-21770-7 (hardcover)
ISBN 978-1-250-24516-8 (signed edition)
ISBN 978-1-250-21769-1 (ebook)

Our books may be purchased in bulk for promotional, educational, or business use. Please contact your local bookseller or the Macmillan Corporate and Premium Sales Department at 1-800-221-7945, extension 5442, or by email at MacmillanSpecialMarkets@macmillan.com.

First Edition: April 2019

10   9   8   7   6   5   4   3   2

To our youngest daughter, Amma,

Whose howl makes me Brave.

And for all of our daughters:

May they live every moment

Knowing the Power of their Wolf

And the Love of their Pack.

Contents

Note to Reader

Since I identify as a woman, this book is written from a woman's point of view. The leadership ideas, however, are universal.

Recently, on a call with a company hiring me to teach about leadership, a man said, "Excuse me, Abby, I just need to ensure that what you present is applicable to men, too."

I said, "Good question! But only if you've asked every male speaker you've hired if his message is applicable to women, too."

Women have had to find themselves within content presented from the male perspective forever. It's essential to flip this and allow men the opportunity to find themselves within content presented from a woman's perspective.

In this book, I use words like *women, men, girls,* and *boys*. These are not my favorite words, as I've always understood gender—even my own—to be on a wide, beautiful spectrum.

My dream is that people of every gender—as well as people between or beyond gender—will find themselves in these pages.

My hope is that this book becomes a leap forward for *humankind*.

WOLFPACK

Welcome to the Wolfpack

Imagine that you've been asked to give a commencement address at one of the premier women's colleges in the nation. You've got fifteen minutes to stand behind a podium in a fancy robe and tell hundreds of brilliant young people everything you know about:

> What makes a good life,
> What makes a beautiful world, and
> How to build both.

Would it make you stop and think hard about what you believe?

Would it make you feel overwhelmed and un-derqualified?

Might it even lead you to sweat profusely and wonder if a person who *hasn't even graduated from college* should really give a commencement speech?

(Maybe that last worry was uniquely mine.)

Shortly after my retirement from soccer, I was asked to deliver such a commencement address at Radio City Music Hall to Barnard College's 126th graduating class.

The invitation said:

> We are awed by your talents on the field, but we are also moved by your commit-ment to issues like gender equality, pay in-equity and gay rights. Our seniors would be thrilled to have you address them at this watershed moment in their lives.

I sat on my couch, read those words twice, and then grabbed my phone and Googled: *watershed moment*. (FYI: It means turning point; historic moment.)

Then I thought:

Ok.

They don't want me to speak as just an athlete.

They want me to speak as an activist, a feminist, a leader.

At one of the most important moments in their lives.

No pressure.

The invitation went on to say:

Former Barnard speakers have included: Barack Obama, Hillary Clinton, Samantha Power, Sheryl Sandberg, Cecile Richards and Meryl Streep.

NBD, I thought. (FYI: For readers over forty, that means No Big Deal.)

Since my retirement, I had been traveling and speaking to people all over the world as a famous athlete. I spoke about my personal life, my time on the field, and how to win championships.

I was a decorated soccer champion.

I'd scored more international goals than any woman or man in history.

I'd won two Olympic gold medals and a FIFA World Cup championship.

That stuff was cool. But since I was a kid, what I loved most about soccer wasn't collecting individual stats or even wins.

I loved winning and losing as ONE team.

I loved being a part of something bigger than myself.

I loved the shared joy, suffering, failure, and success.

I loved the magic of collectively surrendering to an unknown outcome.

I loved the intimacy of our team dinners, bus rides, and stinky locker rooms.

I loved how my teammates and I cared for each other, fought for each other, and respected each other—no matter what.

What I loved most about soccer was being a teammate to women and a leader of women.

As the co-captain of the United States women's national soccer team, I was charged with uniting twenty-three women—each of whom had achieved success because of her individual talent—and inspiring each to commit to the collective. With the help of my teammates, I created a team culture based on more than just excellence. We not only won, we won with joy, honor, connectedness, commitment, and sisterhood. We were not only champions on the field—we were champions of each other. Our time on the U.S. Women's National Team turned us into more than just winners. We turned each other into better friends, citizens, and human beings.

The greatest loss of my retirement was losing my team. I missed the unique connection that is forged among a group of women working toward a collective goal. But as I sat and looked at that invitation, I had this thought:

What if my time on the national team was just practice for a bigger game?

What if I could find a way to translate our team's culture to more women?

What if my new team was All Women Everywhere?

The Barnard women would enter Radio City Music Hall as college students and leave as adults.

What if I entered as Abby, a leader of women on the soccer field, and left as Abby, a leader of women in the world?

I was scared—but I said yes to Barnard anyway.

I said yes for those women, but also for myself. The Barnard women weren't the only ones stepping off into an unknown future, reinventing themselves, trying to find their way in the world. I was right there with them. This speech would be a *watershed moment* for me, too.

First, though, I had to actually write the damn thing.

There was a moment in every soccer game when I'd feel the energy shift toward me. Whether it was a morale boost, a momentum swing, or a goal that we needed—it was my job to make it happen. When I felt that shift, I'd say silently to myself:

Let's go, Abby. It's your time.

As I sat down to prepare my speech, that's what I told myself. I needed this rally cry, because it was a vital and intimidating time in our country to speak for and to women.

The nation was as divided as I've ever known it to be.

White supremacy and misogyny were being legitimized and celebrated at the highest levels of government.

The backlash against progress toward equal justice for all was swift and painful.

The landscape of America was overrun with archaic ways of thinking about gender, race, sexuality, rich and poor, and the environment. Many were angry, and others were numb. Apathy was setting in; effecting any real change felt daunting. It may have felt impossible, even.

Unless, of course, you don't believe in *impossible* because this has been the lesson of your life: A team of women who unite for a larger goal can achieve the impossible again and again.

As I focused on what I wanted to share with the women of Barnard—a directive to unleash their individuality, unite the collective, and change the landscape—my thoughts turned to a TED Talk I'd watched recently about the wolves of Yellowstone National Park.

In 1995, wolves were reintroduced into Yellowstone after being absent for seventy years. It was a controversial decision, but rangers decided it was a risk worth taking, because the land was in trouble.

During those seventy years, the number of deer skyrocketed because they were alone and unchallenged at the top of the food chain. They grazed unchecked and reduced the vegetation so severely that the riverbanks eroded.

Once a small number of wolves arrived, big changes started happening almost immediately.

First, they thinned out the deer through hunting. But more important, the presence of the wolves drastically changed the *behavior* of the remaining deer. Wisely, the deer started avoiding the places they'd be most vulnerable to the wolves—the valleys—and the vegetation in those places regenerated. The height of the trees quintupled in just six years. Birds and beavers started moving in. The beavers built river dams, which provided habitats for otters and ducks and fish. Ravens and bald eagles returned to eat the carrion left by the wolves.

Bears came back because berries started growing again.

But that wasn't all. The *rivers* actually changed as well. The plant regeneration stabilized the riverbanks, so they stopped collapsing. The rivers flowed freely again.

In short:

> The plant ecosystem regenerated.
> The animal ecosystem regenerated.
> The entire landscape changed.
> All because of the wolves' presence.

See what happened there?

The wolves—who were feared by many to be a threat to the system—became the system's *salvation*.

Now, look around our world today: *See what's happening here?*

Women—who are feared by many to be a threat to our system—will become our society's salvation.

We are the ones we've been waiting for.

WE.

ARE.

THE.

WOLVES.

Throughout my life, my Wolfpack was my soccer team.

Now, my Wolfpack is All Women Everywhere.

Wolfpacks need a unifying structure. The most effective way to create a collective heartbeat is to establish rules for the Pack to live by.

The U.S. Women's National Team is a unique thing: an all-women ecosystem separated, in many ways, from the larger system. FIFA (the international governing body of the sport) largely ignores and devalues women's soccer. The women are on their own. They know if they want respect and a future for the sport, they have to create it themselves. They are a pack of wolves hell-bent on changing the landscape of our sport.

In 1999, two years before I joined them, the national team went to FIFA and said: We're going to play in NFL stadiums for the World Cup like the men do.

FIFA said, No. Women don't play in those venues. You'll never sell enough tickets. In other words: Stay in your place. Follow the old rules. Don't be ridiculous. (Note: When they say you're ridiculous, you know you're onto something.)

The U.S. Women's National Team ignored those warnings and set out to build what they dreamed of. They deployed a guerrilla grassroots marketing campaign. They visited schools and spoke to gymnasiums full of kids. They surprised teams of young girls on soccer pitches. They once drove by a youth soccer tournament and asked the bus driver to pull over so they could talk to the kids about the World Cup. They were scrappy and they sacrificed. They were zero ego and all heart. They were united and committed to a vision that they knew was possible and were determined to bring to life.

They did. They sold out stadiums. They created the most powerful women's sports movement the world had ever seen, and the biggest event in the history of women's sports. Their final game, played at the Rose Bowl in Pasadena, was attended by more than 90,000 people—the largest crowd to ever attend a women's sporting event in history. It was also the most-watched soccer game in the U.S. to date, including any men's World Cup matches. With 40 million people around the world watching the game live, it garnered higher ratings than the finals for both professional hockey and basketball. There were suddenly new rules to the game—written by those women—but only because a bunch of badass visionaries had the courage to break the old ones.

As Ava DuVernay, the first black woman to direct a film nominated for an Oscar for Best Picture, said:

Regarding glass ceilings . . . I'm mostly bolstered by folks who create their own ceilings. I'm less interested in banging down the door of some man who doesn't want me there. I'm more about building my own house.

The message I decided to share with the Barnard women—the message of this book—is this: Women must stop following the Old Rules, which exist only to maintain the status quo. If we follow the rules we've always followed, the game will remain the same. Old ways of thinking will never help us build a new world. Out with the Old. In with the New.

Welcome to the Wolfpack Way—8 New Rules that will change the game.

ONE

You Were Always the Wolf

Old Rule: Stay on the path.

New Rule: Create your own path.

Like most little girls, I was taught to keep my head down, stay on the path, and get my job done. I was freaking Little Red Riding Hood.

You know the fairy tale—it's just one iteration of the warning stories girls are told the world over. Little Red Riding Hood heads off through the woods having been given strict instructions: Stay on the path. Don't talk to anybody. Keep your head down and hidden beneath your *Handmaid's Tale* cape.

And she follows the rules . . . at first. But then she dares to get a little curious and she ventures off the path. That's, of course, when she encounters the Big Bad Wolf and all hell breaks loose.

The message of these stories is clear:

> Follow the rules.
> Don't be curious.
> Don't say too much.
> Don't expect more.

Otherwise *bad things will happen*.

But when I look out into the world, as well as back on my life, it becomes clear to me that those stories aren't true. Every good thing that has come to me—and the women I respect—has happened when we dared to venture off the path.

When I was young, I was told: Good girls wear dresses.

I hated wearing dresses.

I'd look at myself in the mirror when I was wearing a dress and the pit in my stomach would rise to my throat. I'd stare at myself and think: I don't like how this looks or how this feels. This is not me.

I felt the need to hold my breath from the second that dress went on until the second I pulled it off. It felt like I was in costume, hiding who I really was in order to fit in, to be good.

Don't we all have a costume we wear to cover our wolf?

The question of my childhood was: Why can't I wear what I want to wear?

When I got to my all-girls high school, the rules seemed to change.

I remember sitting in classrooms witnessing the complete character shifts of some of my friends. Girls who were quiet with our guy friends became animated and opinionated in our all-girls environment. Girls who seldom ate a thing around the boys started chowing down during our lunch periods. And it wasn't just the way we acted and ate that changed without boys around. How we dressed changed, too. At our school, we dressed for comfort, not attention. We learned that girls do not have to dress for boys. We can dress for ourselves. We can wear on the outside how we feel on the inside. We can choose our own comfort even if it makes other people uncomfortable.

I dated boys in high school, because my religious upbringing and culture taught me that this was what girls were supposed to do. Boys were fine, I guess. It wasn't until I felt that spark of infatuation with a girl that I realized love is supposed to be more than just fine. Out of fear of losing my family, I decided that being openly gay wasn't an option for me. This broke my heart.

The question of my teenage years was: Why can't I love who I want to love?

I tried to keep this part of myself buried for as long as I could. Then, during my senior year in high school, I experienced real love for the first time. This love felt as critical and necessary as air, as food, as shelter. I began my first gay relationship like many gay people did back then—in secret. The secrecy felt equal parts enraging and intoxicating. I couldn't tell anyone, so I felt afraid and isolated from my family and friends. But I also learned that real love is a human need and that if I denied myself of it, the wolf inside me would die. Trembling—and secretly for a long while—I chose love. I chose myself.

Later, I began to dream of becoming a professional soccer player. The problem was that women's professional soccer was so new and overlooked that I didn't even know it existed. So I'd watch the U.S. Men's National Team play and think: *But I could do that. I* want *to do that.*

The question of my twenties was: Why can't I become what I want to become?

Little did I know that behind the scenes, women were creating the opportunities that I would one day seize and build my career upon. Women were fighting for Title IX, building professional women's leagues, and striking to ensure a livable wage for the emerging women's national soccer team. By the time I left college, women I'd never met had begun to clear the path I'd walk.

Those women did not Little Red Riding Hood their way through life. There was no path for them, so they made a new one. They laid that new path—brick by brick—for generations of wolves to follow. They created things for me that I didn't even know I needed. They spent their lives and careers building something that many of them knew they'd never get to take advantage of—but they did it anyway.

If I could go back and tell my younger self one thing it would be this:

Abby,
You were never Little Red Riding Hood.
You were always the Wolf.

There is a wolf inside of every woman. Her wolf is who she was made to be before the world told her who to be. Her wolf is her talent, her power, her dreams, her voice, her curiosity, her courage, her dignity, her choices—her truest identity.

CALL TO THE WOLFPACK:

Wear what you want.

Love who you love.

Become what you imagine.

Create what you need.

You were never Little Red Riding Hood.

You were always the Wolf.

TWO

Be Grateful AND Ambitious

Old Rule: Be grateful for what you have.

New Rule: Be grateful for what you have AND demand what you deserve.

When I retired from soccer, ESPN decided to celebrate my career by honoring me with their Icon Award. I'd accept the award at the ESPYS—their nationally televised show—along with two other retiring champions: the NBA's Kobe Bryant and the NFL's Peyton Manning.

I was excited. This felt like a big deal. My first thought was: What am I going to wear?

My answer was—*exactly what I want to wear*—sneakers and all. I got my new suit tailored. I bought some sparkly sneakers. I got my head freshly bleached and shaved. Why not go for soccer icon *and* fashion icon on the same night?

The night of the ESPYS Justin Timberlake, the presenter of our awards, stood on stage and showed highlight videos of our careers to the audience. He talked about what we three had in common: our talent, our grit, our dedication. As he described the lengths we were willing to go, he showed footage of me getting my bloody head stapled back together during a game. He stopped and said, with shock and awe: "They stapled. Her *head*."

The crowd squirmed and laughed, which made me feel like a badass—worthy of the stage I was standing on.

When it was time for us to receive our awards, the three of us stood together while the cameras rolled and the audience cheered. I don't know how Kobe and Peyton felt in that moment, but I felt overwhelming gratitude. I was so grateful to be there—to be included in the company of Kobe and Peyton. I had a momentary feeling of having arrived, like women athletes had finally made it.

Then the applause ended, and it was time for the three of us to exit stage left. As I watched those men walk off the stage, it dawned on me that while the three of us were stepping away from similar careers, we were facing very different futures.

Each of us—Kobe, Peyton, and I—had made the same sacrifices for our careers; shed the same amount of blood, sweat, and tears; won world championships at the same level. We'd left it all on the field for decades with the same ferocity, talent, and commitment. But our retirements wouldn't be the same at all. Because Kobe and Peyton were walking off that stage and into their futures with something I didn't have: enormous bank accounts. Because of that they had something else I didn't have: Freedom. Their hustling days were over. Mine were just beginning.

Later that night, back in my hotel room, I lay in bed and finally acknowledged what had been simmering inside me for decades: Anger.

In the 2018 FIFA Men's World Cup the winning team took home $38 million in prize money—that's nineteen times the amount that the winning team brought home in the 2015 FIFA Women's

World Cup. Nineteen times more. This despite the fact that in 2015, when the U.S. Women's National Team won the World Cup championship, the Women's National Team turned a profit of $6.6 million, whereas the Men's National Team earned a profit of just under $2 million.

I was angry at myself for not speaking up more about this glaring inequity and obvious injustice.

I was angry for my teammates, for my mentors, for all women. Because I knew that this wasn't just about me, and it wasn't just about sports.

My story is every woman's story.

On average, women across the globe will earn significantly less than men in equivalent positions throughout their careers. In the first quarter of 2018, women in the U.S. earned 81.1 percent of what their male counterparts earned across all industries and ages. Studies have shown that, on average, women must work sixty-six extra days in order to earn the same salary as their male counterparts. Wage inequity is even more devastating for women of color: Black women are typically paid only 63 cents, and Latina women only 54 cents, for every dollar paid to their white, male counterparts.

I spent most of my time during my career the same way I'd spent my time on that ESPYS stage. Just feeling grateful. I was so grateful for a paycheck, so grateful to represent my country, so grateful to be the token woman at the table, so grateful to receive any respect at all that I was afraid to use my voice to demand more for myself—and equality for all of us.

What keeps the pay gap in existence is not just the entitlement and complicity of men. It's the gratitude of women.

Our gratitude is how power uses the tokenism of a few women to keep the rest of us in line.

CALL TO THE WOLFPACK:

Be grateful.

But do not JUST be grateful.

Be grateful AND brave.

Be grateful AND ambitious.

Be grateful AND righteous.

Be grateful AND persistent.

Be grateful AND loud.

Be grateful for what you have AND demand what you deserve.

THREE

Lead from the Bench

Old Rule: Wait for permission to lead.

New Rule: Lead now—from wherever you are.

When we think of leaders, who do we imagine? Politicians? CEOs? Coaches?

I know that's who I usually think of. Here's my question: Why don't we think of ourselves?

Maybe because our cultural understanding of leadership has omitted far too many of us for far too long.

2015 was a big year for me. It would be the last year of my career, and I was planning to go out with a bang by leading the U.S. Women's National Team to a World Cup championship.

As co-captain, part of my job was to help the

coaching staff assemble the eleven starters who would give us the best chance to win the tournament.

Hard decisions needed to be made.

After the first few games, it became clear that I didn't belong on that starting roster anymore. At thirty-five, I was one of the oldest players on the team. I had lost a step and I was suffering from chronic pain. I wasn't the player I used to be. The team knew it, the coaches knew it, I knew it.

So imagine this: You've scored more international goals in your sport than any human being on the planet. You've co-captained and led Team USA to victory after victory for the past decade. And you and your coach sit down and decide together that you won't be a starter for the remainder of your final World Cup. Instead, you'll come off the bench.

This was hard to accept as Abby Wambach, co-captain of Team USA. It was even harder to accept as Abby, the competitive kid who dreamed of finishing her career the way she'd played it, leading her team to victory on the field.

But finishing my career as a starter wouldn't have taught me the most important lesson of leadership, the one I had yet to learn, the one that would carry me into the next phase of my life. I knew how to lead on the field. Now I needed to learn how to lead from the bench.

The second game of the tournament arrived. I was accustomed to walking out onto the field in front of the roaring crowd while holding the hand of a wide-eyed kid, in line with the other starters. We'd walk to the center of the field, face the flags, and listen to our country's anthem. This was my pregame ritual and one of the honors of my career. But this time I walked into the stadium with the reserve players, stopped in front of our bench—and watched another set of eleven players put their hands over their hearts for the anthem.

I knew that the eyes of the crowd, my teammates, and my fans were on me. They were all watching to see how I would react. I had a choice between pouting and making this moment about me or swallowing my pride and making it about our team.

When I was on the field, what inspired and motivated me most was not the millions of strangers cheering but when my *teammates* paid attention, saw me, and believed in me. I thought of my longtime teammate and friend Lori Lindsey. We'd played together since we were fifteen years old. Lori wasn't a consistent starter on the national team, but she made our team better because she put as much energy into cheering from the bench as some players did when they played ninety minutes. So I channeled Lori.

I paid attention. I screamed so loudly, obnoxiously, and relentlessly that the coach moved me to the far side of the bench. I kept water ready for players coming off the field. I celebrated when goals were scored, and I kept believing in us even when mistakes were made. I knew the women on the field like sisters, so I could predict, in every moment, exactly what each needed from me. Whatever it was—comfort, encouragement, tough love, instruction—I offered it. At the end of that game, I was so exhausted, it was like I'd played all ninety minutes. The starters had left it all on the field; I'd left it all on the bench.

I did that again and again throughout the entire tournament. We won the World Cup that year. We celebrated together—starters and bench players—as one team. I know in my bones that one of the reasons we won the 2015 World Cup was the support of the bench. The pride I feel about how I handled that tournament rivals the pride I have about scoring any big goal.

You'll feel benched sometimes, too. You'll find yourself taken off the project, passed over for the promotion, falling sick, losing the election, side-lined by the kid who doesn't seem to need you anymore. You might find yourself holding a baby instead of a briefcase and fearing that your colleagues are "getting ahead" and leaving you behind.

Here's what's important: You are allowed to be disappointed when it feels like life's benched you. What you aren't allowed to do is miss your opportunity to lead from the bench.

If you're not a leader on the bench, don't call yourself a leader on the field.

You're either a leader everywhere or nowhere.

By the way, the fiercest leaders I've ever seen have been parents. Parenting is no bench—it just might be the big game.

Every woman is the leader of her own life. Do not give up that power. Claim it. Value it. Use it.

The picture of leadership is not just a man at the head of a table. It's also every woman who is allowing her *own voice* to guide her life and the lives of those she cares about.

Leadership is volunteering at the local school, speaking encouraging words to a friend, and holding the hand of a dying parent. It's tying dirty shoelaces and going to therapy and saying to our families and friends: *No. We don't do unkindness here.* It's signing up to run for the school board and it's driving that single mom's kid home from practice and it's creating boundaries that prove to the world that you value yourself. Leadership is taking care of yourself and empowering others to do the same.

Leadership is not a position to earn, it's an inherent power to claim.

Leadership is the blood that runs through your veins—it's born in you.

It's not the privilege of a few, it is the right and responsibility of all.

Leader is not a title that the world gives to you—it's an offering that you give to the world.

CALL TO THE WOLFPACK:

If you have a voice, you have influence to spread.

If you have relationships, you have hearts to guide.

If you know young people, you have futures to mold.

If you have privilege, you have power to share.

If you have money, you have support to give.

If you have a ballot, you have policy to shape.

If you have pain, you have empathy to offer.

If you have freedom, you have others to fight for.

If you are alive, you are a leader.

FOUR

Make Failure Your Fuel

Old Rule: Failure means you're out of the game.

New Rule: Failure means you're finally IN the game.

When I was on the youth national team and dreaming of one day playing alongside Mia Hamm, I had the opportunity to visit the locker room of the U.S. Women's National Team. Time stopped for me as I looked around and tried to memorize everything I saw: my heroes' grass-stained cleats, their names and numbers hanging above their lockers, their uniforms folded neatly on their chairs.

But the image that stayed with me forever was something else entirely.

What I remember most vividly is a 5×7 photograph.

Someone had taped this small picture next

to the door so it would be the last thing every player saw before she headed out to the training field.

You might guess that it was a picture of a celebration, the team cheering their last big win or standing on a podium accepting gold medals. But it wasn't. It was a picture of their longtime rival— the Norwegian national team—celebrating after having just beaten the USA in the 1995 World Cup. It was a picture of their own team's last defeat.

Five years later, I was called up to that national team. One day we were on the road with nothing to do but sit around a big table in the dining hall and pass around stories for hours. I mustered up the courage to ask about that picture. I needed to know what it meant to them, so I asked:

"Hey, what was the deal with the picture you kept on the locker room wall of the Norwegian team? Why did you want that to be the last thing you looked at before you went out to play?"

They smiled, and it became clear to me that they'd been waiting for the rookie to start asking the right questions. They began to explain to me that the first order of national team business is to win. But that when failure does come, the team isn't afraid of it; the team is fueled by it. The team never denies its last failure. We don't reject it. We don't accept it as proof that we aren't worthy of playing at the highest level. Instead, we insist upon remembering. Because we know that the lessons of yesterday's loss become the fuel for tomorrow's win.

I asked, "Do you think putting that picture up worked?"

Julie Foudy said, "Well, we brought home our first Olympic gold the following year. What do you think?"

I left that table understanding that in order to become a champion—on and off the field—I'd need to spend my life transforming my failures into my fuel.

Women haven't yet accessed the power of failure. When it comes, we panic, deny it, or reject it outright. Worst-case scenario, we view failure as proof that we were always unworthy imposters. Men have been allowed to fail and keep playing forever. Why do we let failure take us out of the game?

Imperfect men have been empowered and permitted to run the world since the beginning of time. It's time for imperfect women to grant themselves permission to join them.

Perfection is not a prerequisite of leadership. But we can forgive ourselves for believing it is.

We've been living by the old rules that insist that a woman must be perfect before she's worthy of showing up. Since no one is perfect, this rule is an effective way to keep women out of leadership preemptively.

It's time for a new rule.

Women must stop accepting failure as our destruction and start using failure as our fuel. Failure is not something to be ashamed of—nor is it proof of unworthiness. Failure is something to be *powered* by.

When we live afraid to fail, we don't take risks. We don't bring our entire selves to the table—so we end up failing before we even begin.

Let's stop worrying: *What if I fail?* Instead, let's promise ourselves: *When I fail, I'll stick around.*

After I retired from playing, I was hired by ESPN to commentate the men's 2016 UEFA European Championship—an internationally televised soccer tournament. I traveled to Paris, settled into my hotel, and showed up the first day feeling nervous and excited. The second the red "on air" light turned on, my brain turned off. The other commentators easily conversed about players, stats, and systems. I couldn't even remember how to speak. Within the first five minutes I could tell that I was in way over my head. When I checked my Twitter feed it became clear that the rest of the world could tell, too. I had failed. My embarrassment burned.

I was tempted to get on the first flight home. I kept showing up and saw the tournament through to the end, but it was brutal.

On the flight home, I felt sick. I kept thinking: *Commentating is what former athletes do. After failing at this, are there any options left for me?* I went home and sat with this fear for a long time. Eventually, I decided that I had two options. I could use this public failure as a career-ending excuse or I could use it as helpful information. I could take from this experience that I was destined to be a failure, or I could take from it that I wasn't—*at this moment*—destined to be a commentator. I crossed commentator off my list and kept throwing darts. A few months later, I founded my leadership company. Every day now, I do what I love—teaching emerging leaders how to become champions for themselves and others. That commentating failure didn't end my career—it helped me find my career. Sometimes we use failure to push us further down the same path. Other times, we let failure guide us to a new path. But we always keep moving forward.

The world needs to see women take risks, fail big, and insist on their right to stick around and try again. And again. And again. A champion never allows a short-term failure to take her out of the long-term game. A woman who doesn't give up can never lose.

CALL TO THE WOLFPACK:

Try.

Fail.

Feel it burn.

Then transform Failure into your Fuel.

FIVE

Champion Each Other

Old Rule: Be against each other.

New Rule: Be FOR each other.

During every ninety-minute soccer game there are a few magical moments when the ball actually hits the back of the net and a goal is scored. When this happens, it means that everything has come together perfectly—the perfect pass, the perfectly timed run, every player in the precise place at exactly the right time—culminating in a moment in which one player scores that goal.

What happens next on the field is what transforms a group of individual women into one team. The bench erupts. Teammates from all over the field rush toward the goal scorer. There are high fives, chest bumps, dances, hugs, and a spontaneous celebratory huddle that disperses as quickly as it began.

It might appear to the crowd that the team is celebrating the goal scorer, but what the team is *really* celebrating is every player, every coach, every practice, every sprint, every doubt, and every failure that this one single goal represents.

Sometimes you will make a sixty-yard sprint only to watch another woman score the big goal. Sometimes it was your tackle, your run, your heart, and your sweat that made that goal possible.

You will not always be the goal scorer. When you are not, you better be rushing toward her.

Sometimes you *will* be the goal scorer.

I was that goal scorer 184 times during my international career.

If you watch footage of any of those goals, you'll see that the moment after I score, I begin to point.

I point to the teammate who assisted.

I point to the defender who protected us.

I point to the midfielder who ran tirelessly.

I point to the coach who dreamed up this play.

I point to the bench player who willed this moment into existence.

I've never scored a goal in my life without getting a pass from someone else.

Every goal I've ever scored belonged to my entire team.

When you score, you better start pointing.

When a woman scores, there are only two options for the Wolfpack:

We're either rushing or we're pointing.

Here's what rushing and pointing look like off the field:

> We amplify each other's voices.
> We demand seats for women, people
>   of color, and all marginalized people
>   at every table where decisions are
>   made.
> We celebrate each other's successes.

We express gratitude and give credit
to those who contributed to our
own successes.
And when one of us falls, we support
her rise.

When we encounter women who are still living by the old rules, instead of fighting against them, we continue to fight for all.

Championing each other can be difficult for women because for so long we have been pitted against each other for the token seat at the table. Maintaining the illusion of scarcity is how power keeps women competing for the singular seat at the old table, instead of uniting and building a new, bigger table.

Scarcity has been planted inside of us and among us. This is not our fault—but it is our problem to solve.

Revolutions begin with a collective belief.

The Wolfpack's belief is that scarcity is a lie.

That power and success and joy are not pies. A bigger slice for one woman doesn't mean a smaller slice for another. We believe that love, justice, success, and power are infinite and meant to be accessible to all.

Revolutions are won with collective action.

We will take action on behalf of all of us.

We will help each other. We will rush toward each other. We will point to each other. We will claim infinite joy, success, and power—together. We will celebrate the success of one woman as a collective success for all women.

CALL TO THE WOLFPACK:

Her victory is your victory. Celebrate with her.

Your victory is her victory. Point to her.

SIX

Demand the Ball

Old Rule: Play it safe. Pass the ball.

New Rule: Believe in yourself.
Demand the ball.

When I was a younger player, my heroes were the women of the national team. Among them was Michelle Akers, the best player in the world. Michelle was tall like I am, built like I'd be built, and the most courageous soccer player I'd ever seen play. She personified every one of my dreams.

Since there was no professional women's league at the time, Michelle had to find different ways to train between national team games. So one day our youth national team found ourselves preparing to play alongside our hero. We were eighteen years old and there was Michelle Akers—a chiseled powerhouse of a woman, a world champion, a legend. Our hands shook as we laced up our cleats.

We were playing a scrimmage—five against

five. For the first three quarters of play, Michelle was taking it easy on us, coaching us, teaching us about spacing, timing, and the tactics of the game.

At the start of the fourth quarter, Michelle realized that because of all of this coaching, her team was losing by three goals. In that moment, we saw a light switch on inside of her.

She ran back to her own goalkeeper, stood one yard away from her, and screamed:

GIVE. ME. THE. EFFING. BALL.

The goalkeeper gave her the effing ball.

And Michelle took that ball and dribbled through our entire effing team and she scored.

This game was "winners keepers," meaning that if you scored, you got the ball back. So after Michelle scored, the ball went right back to her goalkeeper.

And so did Michelle. She ran back to her goalie, and again stood a yard away from her and screamed:

GIVE ME THE BALL.

The keeper gave her the ball.

And again Michelle dribbled through us and scored.

And then she did it again. And again. Until she'd taken her team to victory.

What I saw in Michelle that day changed how I saw myself forever.

Before that game, I had always tried to turn down my talent and dim my light to avoid outshining others. I thought it was the humble thing to do. I was afraid that my talent would be an affront to others and might drive a wedge between my teammates and me. So on the field, I operated at 75 percent.

But watching Michelle, I saw the power of one woman's competitive fire. I saw a woman who not only wanted to win, but owned that desire, and believed that she could be the one to make it happen.

That game marked the moment I stopped pretending to be less powerful than I know I am.

What I learned is that the most inspiring thing on earth is a woman who believes in herself, who gives 100 percent, and who owns her greatness unapologetically.

Watching Michelle use her power shamelessly freed me to use mine, too.

I think about Michelle every time I'm tempted to decide I'm unworthy, unprepared, incapable, or not good enough.

Three years ago, I fell in love with a woman who has three children. I'd always wanted to be a mother, but I felt completely unprepared to be a *step*mother. I kept coming back to the horror stories I'd heard about stepmothers and their children. I felt afraid that the kids would resent me and would never see me as their true parent. I worried I'd be incapable of earning their love and respect, arriving this far down the road of their lives. I was most scared for myself—that I might never feel the love a biological parent feels for their children. Would I be good enough? I didn't know.

But I decided that when you want something as badly as I wanted a life with Glennon—when you want something as badly as I wanted a family—you just have to show up before you're ready and demand the effing ball.

I married Glennon, and I became a stepparent. Chase, Tish, and Amma call me their "bonus mom." Becoming Glennon's wife and my children's bonus mom was the best decision I've ever made in my life. Is it easy? Hell no. Every day I have moments filled with doubt about my parenting decisions—but Glennon promises me that constant doubt isn't unique to stepparenting—it's just the parenting condition. Glennon, her ex-husband Craig, and I are a Pack. We threw away the old stories about blended families and decided to write a new one. Our themes are respect, grace, and the constant decision to value collective peace over our individual egos.

Sometimes I look at my family and think: What if I'd decided not to become a mother until I felt ready, or until I'd secured certainty that I'd never make a mistake? I'd have missed the best thing that's ever happened to me. I also would have missed my opportunity to help other families like mine. Every day I hear from people who are using our family as inspiration to write their own unique and beautiful stories about blended families.

In the end, owning and unleashing all your power isn't just about you. It's also about the domino effect. When you stand up and demand the ball, you give others permission to do the same. The Wolfpack's collective power begins by unleashing the power of each individual Wolf.

As it says in *The Jungle Book*:

The strength of the Pack is the Wolf, and the strength of the Wolf is the Pack.

CALL TO THE WOLFPACK:

Believe in yourselves.

Stand up and say:

GIVE ME THE EFFING BALL.

GIVE ME THE EFFING JOB.

GIVE ME THE SAME PAY THAT THE GUY NEXT TO ME GETS.

GIVE ME THE PROMOTION.

GIVE ME THE MICROPHONE.

GIVE ME THE OVAL OFFICE.

GIVE ME THE RESPECT I DESERVE—

AND GIVE IT TO MY WOLFPACK, TOO.

SEVEN

Bring It All

Old Rule: Lead with dominance.
Create Followers.

New Rule: Lead with humanity.
Cultivate Leaders.

When Pia Sundhage was hired as our new coach for the national team, we were the biggest, fittest, strongest, most physically dominant team in the world. We were winning by the sheer force of power and intimidation alone. That was fine with us. The score at the end of the game was the only thing that mattered, full stop.

The first time Pia met with us, she said:

You are the best in the world. But there is still a higher level in you. You have proven you can win games. What I want you to work on is how you win games. I want us to continue to win, but I want us to win while honoring ourselves, our teammates, our opponents, and the game. We will

win with creativity, innovation, and steady as-
suredness instead of just physical dominance. We
will win beautifully.

Then she pulled out a guitar and began to sing "The Times They Are A-Changin'" by Bob Dylan.

Our team sat there, stunned. We stared at this Swedish woman thinking: *She has absolutely no idea what she's doing. We're screwed.*

This was the first time many of us had ever seen a leader make herself vulnerable. We didn't even know that was allowed—it felt, at first, like a leadership breach. And yet, as we listened to her sing, though we felt a little awkward, we became curious. Soon, we felt moved. We felt a part of ourselves awaken. We felt connected.

Pia brought music to us because Pia loves music. By showing us who she was and what she loved, she taught us that real leaders know who they are and bring every bit of themselves to whomever they lead. Real leaders don't mimic a cultural construct of what a leader looks, sounds, and acts like. They understand that there are as many authentic ways to lead as there are people.

Looking back, I can see that Pia's impromptu musical performance was the catalyst our team needed to begin reimagining our ideas about how to lead, and about who gets to lead.

Before Pia, we subscribed to the old, top-down structure of leadership. Wisdom, direction, and ideas were determined and announced by the coaches and captains, and immediately, without questions or input, executed by the team. Before Pia, our team was made up of a few leaders and dozens of followers. After Pia, our leadership structure was slowly broken down and re-created. Off the field, my role as co-captain became less about making pronouncements *to* everyone and more about eliciting ideas *from* everyone. Players began to feel safe and brave enough to bring their voices and ideas to the table. On the field, we started coaching each other. The new kid, Alex Morgan, started giving me pointers. Veterans began to learn from newbies, starters began to learn from bench players. Captains began to learn from the strength and conditioning coaches. Every single person—from players to support staff—began to think of themselves as a leader.

This new way wasn't always comfortable. It required courage from the new players and humility from folks, like me, who were used to telling, not listening. But we had Pia as a model. This new way wasn't just a theory to us. If Pia had just *told* us to be brave, humble, and vulnerable, we would never have been able to embody it. As our leader, she had to *show* us.

The old way is to lead with invulnerability and enlist followers.

The new way is to lead with full humanity—and cultivate a team of leaders.

CALL TO THE WOLFPACK:

Claim your power, and bring along your full humanity.

Clear the way for others to do the same.

Because what our families,

our companies,

and the world needs

is nothing more—and nothing less—

than exactly who we are.

EIGHT

Find Your Pack

Old Rule: You're on your own.

New Rule: You're not alone. You've got your Pack.

After I retired, I gave my body a three-year detox from any kind of punishing physical activity. When I felt ready to begin again, I decided to join my friend Mel in a running challenge. We committed to running on our own every day and sending each other our distances for accountability. After thirty years of training, I figured that this challenge would be a piece of cake—and help me burn off all the actual pieces of cake I've thoroughly enjoyed in retirement.

The challenge was not a piece of cake. It was miserable. I hated every single minute of every single run. It was like I had lead in my feet, like I'd never run before. My survival mantra as I gasped for air was: *This hurts. This hurts. Don't stop. Don't stop.*

One night, I said to Glennon, "Listen, I've never liked running, but I've also never hated it this much. Why does it feel so impossible all of a sudden? I was a professional athlete! I used to train six hours a day! Could I have lost all of my athleticism in three years?"

She said, "Babe, you haven't lost your athleticism. The difference is that you don't have your teammates running with you anymore. You used to run with your Pack. Now you're a lone wolf out there."

She was right. My entire life I'd been surrounded by teammates suffering with me, encouraging me, making me laugh, and pulling me out of my own head. Our suffering was lessened because we shared it. Life is harder as a lone wolf. We all need a Pack.

When Barnard posted my Wolfpack speech online, it went viral.

Women I've admired my entire life—world leaders, celebrities, athletes, and activists—shared my words with their communities. People circulated it to their companies, schools, friend groups, and classrooms. Parents turned my speech into art and hung paintings of wolves on their daughters' bedroom walls.

What impacted me most was not how wide the speech went—but how deep it went.

I've saved messages like this one to read when I'm tempted to forget that showing up matters.

Abby, When I watched your speech, I realized that you were saying things I'd felt my entire life but didn't have words to explain. I've stopped reading old fairy tales with my daughters. Your speech is our new bedtime story. My hope is that yours is the new message my girls believe about who they are and who they can be. I want them to believe that they are the Wolves: and that they can create their own Pack. Honestly, I want to believe it, too. My entire life I've been the only one. The only woman in the room, the only woman at the table, and I've raised my daughters without a village. Being a woman is a special kind of lonely. We are siloed into our little spaces, isolated from each other. Men have the old boys' club. We need one. I want a Wolfpack for me, too.

Whether you're a mom, a college student, a CEO, or a little girl, you need a crew of brave and honest women to support you. You need them to hold you accountable to your greatness, remind you of who you are, and join you to change the world.

You need a Pack.

The question is: How do we build one?

I know from my career that when you're new at anything—when you don't know what to do or how to begin—all you can do is show up, awkwardly and nervously sometimes, and try.

So I'm going to try. I'm going to gather the

women I respect, admire, and trust most. I'm going to support them when they need it and ask them for help when I need it.

Together, we will change our lives and our world by knowing the power of our Wolf and the strength of our Pack.

Abby Wambach

CALL TO THE WOLFPACK:

Life is not meant to be lived as a

Lone Wolf.

We all need a Pack.

Time to Change the Game

On the night of my final game, after seventeen years as a collegiate, professional, and national team player, I decided to release a farewell message to the sport to which I had given so much of my life—and to the players, teams, and fans who had given so much of their lives to me.

My final message to the game: *Forget Me*.

It aired on television the night I retired. In it, I sat on a metal chair cleaning out my locker, pondering the legacy I'd leave. The screen flashed with images of little girls scoring goals, young women running sprints, and a teenage boy wearing my jersey.

While the clips rolled, I said this:

Forget me. Forget my number. Forget my name. Forget I ever existed.

Forget the medals won, the records broken, and the sacrifices made.

I want to leave a legacy where the ball keeps rolling forward. Where the next generation accomplishes things so great that I am no longer remembered.

So—Forget me. Because the day I'm forgotten is the day we will succeed.

My dream was to leave a legacy ensuring the future success of the sport I'd dedicated my life to. I wanted little girls coming up after me to accomplish things I'd only dreamed of.

A year later, I found myself coaching my ten-year-old daughter's soccer team. As a matter of fact, I coached them all the way to the championship. I didn't talk about my career much because I was committed to keeping the focus on them—but I secretly enjoyed that these kids knew an Olympian was leading them.

Then one day, near the end of our season, when I was warming the team up and telling a story about my retirement, one of my players looked up at me and said, "So what did you retire from?"

I paused for a moment, wondering if she was joking. She wasn't.

I looked down at her and I said, "Um. SOC-CER."

And she said, "Oh. Who did you play for?"

I widened my eyes and said, "THE. UNITED. STATES. OF. AMERICA."

And she said, "Huh. Cool. Wait . . . does that mean you know Alex Morgan?!!"

Be careful what you wish for. They forgot me.

Seriously, though, others not knowing who I was didn't bother me.

What scared me to death was that after retiring, *I* didn't know who I was.

When I took off my jersey for the last time, I lost the identity that I'd proudly worn since I was five years old: Abby Wambach, soccer player.

Without soccer: Who was I?

One night I told Glennon how afraid I was that when I lost soccer, I'd lost myself. The next day, she wrote me this:

Abby, What is most special about you isn't your talent on the soccer field.

When people look at you, they notice something about you that's different.

It's the way you carry yourself and the way you treat people. It's about your dignity mixed with your ferocity. It's about your particular beauty that stands in stark contrast to the manufactured beauty that women have been sold. It's about how you stand and run and talk.

It's a little bit about your hair.

You are a walking glorious rebellion. What you release into the world rekindles a fire inside of us that the world put out long ago.

I don't think the magic was on the field, Abby. I think the magic is inside of you. I think you'll carry it with you till you die. From out here, Abby, it is crystal clear that soccer didn't make you special—you made soccer special. You have lost nothing. You take it all with you. Soccer led us to you. Now we'll follow. Not because of you as an athlete, because of you, my Abby.

She was right. You know who I am now? I'm still the same Abby. I still show up and give 100 percent—now to my new Pack—and I still fight every day to make a better future for the next generation.

You see, soccer didn't make me who I am. I brought who I am to soccer, and I get to bring who I am wherever I go.

So do you.

So don't just ask yourself, "What do I want to do?" Ask yourself: "*Who* do I want to be?"

The most important thing I've learned is that what you do will never define you for long. Who you are always will.

We are the Wolves.

There is magic inside of us.

There is power among us.

Let's unleash and unite.

Let's storm these valleys together, and change the game forever.

NEW RULES

1. Create your own path.

2. Be grateful for what you have AND demand what you deserve.

3. Lead now—from wherever you are.

4. Failure means you're finally IN the game.

5. Be FOR each other.

6. Believe in yourself. Demand the ball.

7. Lead with humanity. Cultivate Leaders.

8. You're not alone. You've got your Pack.

About the Author

Abby Wambach is a two-time Olympic gold medalist, FIFA World Cup champion, and the highest all-time international goal scorer for male and female soccer players. She is an activist for equality and inclusion and the *New York Times* bestselling author of *Forward: A Memoir.* Abby is co-founder of Wolfpack Endeavor, which is revolutionizing leadership development for women in the workplace and beyond through her champion mind-set, individualized coaching, and team-bound focus.

Abby lives in Florida with her wife and three children.